Linking art to the world around us

Arty Facts

Insects, Bugs,
& Art Activities

🌳 Crabtree Publishing Company
www.crabtreebooks.com

Crabtree Publishing Company

PMB 16A, 350 Fifth Avenue, Suite 3308
New York, NY
10118

612 Welland Avenue
St. Catharines, Ontario
L2M 5V6

Coordinating Editor: Ellen Rodger
Project Editors: P.A. Finlay, Carrie Gleason
Production Coordinator: Rosie Gowsell
Proofreading, Indexing: Wendy Scavuzzo

Project Development and Concept Marshall Direct:
Editorial Project Director: Karen Foster
Editors: Claire Sippi, Hazel Songhurst, Samantha Sweeney
Researchers: Gerry Bailey, Alec Edgington
Design Director: Tracy Carrington
Designers: Flora Awolaja, Claire Penny, Paul Montague,
James Thompson, Mark Dempsey,
Production: Edward MacDermott, Victoria Grimsell, Christina Brown
Photo Research: Andrea Sadler
Illustrator: Jan Smith
Model Artists: Sue Partington, Abigail Dean

Prepress, printing and binding by Worzalla Publishing Company

Cataloging in Publication Data
Parker, Steve.
   Insects, bugs, and art activities / written by Steve Parker & Polly Goodman.
      p. cm. -- (Arty facts)
   Information about various topics related to honeybees, caterpillars, dragonflies, snails
and other insects and invertebrates forms the foundation for a variety of craft projects.
   ISBN 0-7787-1137-4 (pbk) -- ISBN 0-7787-1109-9 (RLB)
   1. Insects--Juvenile literature. 2. Invertebrates--Juvenile literature. 3. Insects--Study
and teaching (Elementary)--Activity programs. 4. Invertebrates--Study and teaching
(Elementary)--Activity programs. [1. Insects. 2. Invertebrates. 3. Handicraft.]
I. Goodman,Polly. II. Title. III. Series.
   QL467.2 .P354 2002
   595.7--dc21   2002019257
                                                       LC

Created by
Marshall Direct Learning
© 2002 Marshall Direct Learning

FRONT COVER IMAGES: RICHARD SHELL/ OXFORD SCIENTIFIC FILMS; CNRI/ SCIENCE PHOTO LIBRARY; DAVID DENNIS/ OXFORD SCIENTIFIC FILMS; NIGEL CATTLIN/ HOLT STUDIOS

Linking art to the world around us

Arty Facts

Insects, Bugs
& Art Activities

Contents

Polka dots

L adybugs are small beetles with a round red, orangey-red, or black body covered with black, white, or red spots. There are more than 4,000 different **species**, or kinds, of ladybugs living all over the world. Farmers and gardeners welcome them because they are helpful **insects**. Ladybugs feed on **aphids** and insects which damage crops. One tiny ladybug can eat up to 100 aphids a day!

A long sleep

To stay alive during the cold winter months, ladybugs **hibernate**, or sleep, until the spring. Every autumn, large groups of ladybugs gather together close to where they will hibernate. These places are usually where the ladybugs will be sheltered from the weather – under stones, or tree roots. Some species collect in such large numbers that they take over an area. The average number of two-spotted ladybirds in a group, for example, is about 1,000.

Spot count

There are two-spotted, seven-spotted, nine-spotted, ten-spotted, and even thirteen-spotted ladybugs. The spots may look like decoration, but they have an important purpose. Together with the ladybug's red wings, the spot pattern warns hungry **predators** that the ladybug will taste horrible! Ladybugs ooze a bad tasting yellow blood from their knee joints. So, once a bird has eaten one kind of ladybug, it will never touch another one again!

Insects & Bugs

Ladybug racetrack

1 Cut out a variety of leaf shapes from tissue paper and flower shapes from the gold paper.

2 Glue five leaf pattern lanes on poster board. Number each leaf.

3 Paint five matchboxes different colors.

4 Glue your boxes on the poster board at the finishing line of the game.

5 Draw and cut out a shape like this from poster board. Fold along the dotted lines.

6 Fold up and glue the shape to make a dice. Stick on sequins for the dots. From the poster board make five ladybug counters for each matchbox.

Play this game with two or more friends

To play: Choose a lane and throw a six to start a counter. If you land on a flower, the counter goes back to the beginning. The winner is the first player to get all five ladybug counters in their matchbox.

5

Honeycombs

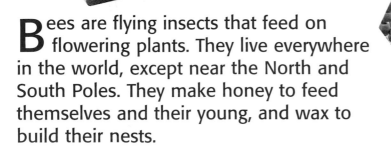

Honey bees depositing nectar and pollen in the honeycomb.

Wax nests

The wax nests are called honeycombs. There are about 20,000 different species of bees in the world, but only the honey bee makes enough honey and wax for people to use.

Busy colonies

Honey bees live and work together in large groups, called **colonies**. Each colony has one queen bee and thousands of female worker bees. There are also hundreds of male bees, called **drones**. Each bee has a special job. The queen bee's only job is to lay eggs. The male drones mate with the queen. The worker bees collect food and build the honeycomb.

Building the honeycomb

The honeycomb is often built inside the hollow of a tree. It is made up of many six-sided, or hexagonal, cells. The worker bees produce the wax from special **glands** on their bodies. The cells are used for the eggs and **larvae**, and to store **pollen** and honey.

Special food

Worker bees collect pollen. They also suck liquid **nectar** from flowers, which they store in their stomachs. They put the nectar and pollen in the honeycomb, where the nectar turns into honey. The honey feeds the workers and the bee larvae growing in the **comb**. For the first three days, young bees are fed a special food called **royal jelly**. This is the only food fed to young queen bees.

Bees are flying insects that feed on flowering plants. They live everywhere in the world, except near the North and South Poles. They make honey to feed themselves and their young, and wax to build their nests.

Honey bee home

WHAT YOU NEED

poster board

scissors

pencil

paint and brush

tape

ruler

glue

yarn

tissue paper

1 Draw and cut out five hexagonal shapes from poster board.

2 Fold into shape along the dotted lines, as shown.

3 Secure flaps with tape.

4 Glue the five shapes together and paint them.

5 Draw and paint bees on poster board and cut them out.

6 Cut out and glue on tissue-paper wings.

7 Tape a piece of yarn to each bee and hang inside the honeycomb.

Decorate the honeycomb with paper leaves

Glass wings

Dragonflies are beautiful fast-flying insects with a colorful slender body and four lacy wings. They have large **compound eyes**, made up of many tiny lenses, or facets, which help them spot their **prey** up to 20 feet (6 m) away. Dragonflies live close to rivers, lakes, and ponds, where they hover and dart through the air, catching smaller insects for food.

Growing up

Dragonflies grow in three stages, changing from an egg to a **nymph**, and then to a fully grown adult. The female lays her eggs in shallow water, or on a water plant. After one or two weeks, the egg **hatches** into a nymph that looks more like a fish than an insect. It has no wings and breathes through gills. A nymph eats insects and small water animals. The nymph lives underwater for one to five years. As it slowly grows, the nymph sheds its skin, or **molts**, about twelve times. When it finally leaves the water, the nymph molts one last time. It is now a fully grown dragonfly.

Speedy wings

The dragonfly's large wings and thin body make it the fastest-flying insect. It can reach speeds of 56 miles per hour (90 km/h) which helps it to catch prey, but also to escape from **predators**, such as birds. Dragonflies beat their shimmering, gauzy wings up and down one pair at a time, up to 100 times a second. A dragonfly's body can be green, red, or blue with black, yellow, or white patterns on it.

Dragonfly fan

poster
board

glue

net fabric

pencil

sequins

paints and
brush

scissors

1 Draw a dragonfly body and wings on poster board and cut them out.

2 Cover the wings with netting and paint them.

3 Paint the body and decorate with glittery sequins. Glue on large sequins for the eyes.

4 Glue the wings onto the body.

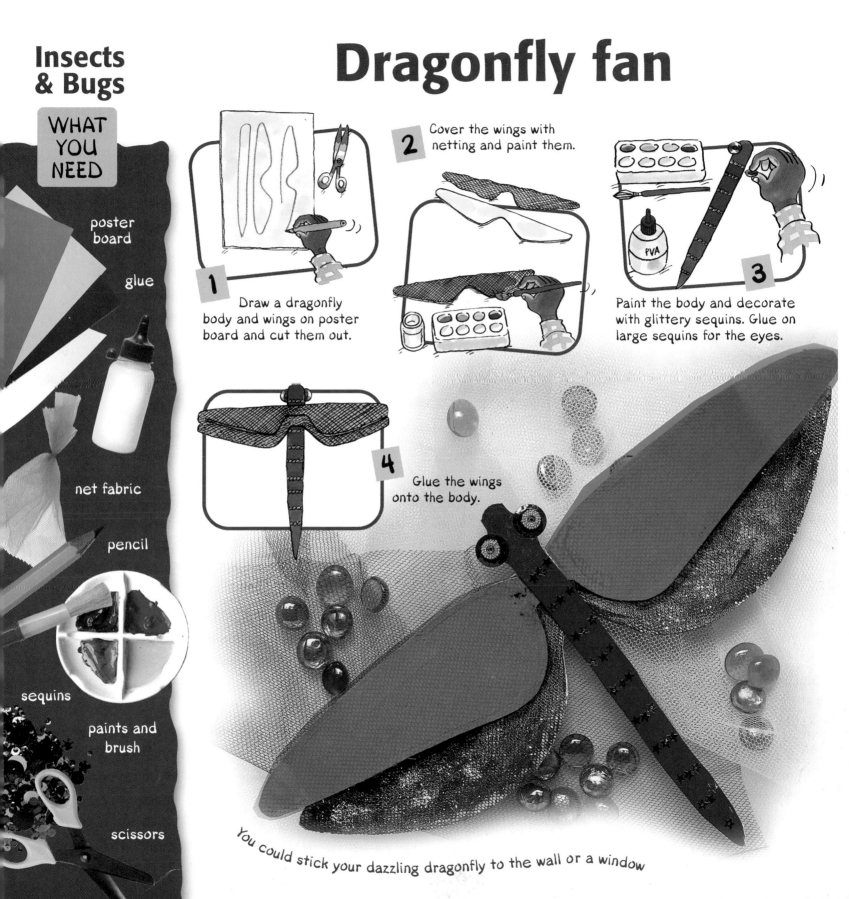

You could stick your dazzling dragonfly to the wall or a window

Caterpillars

Caterpillars are the second stage in the life of butterflies and moths. When a butterfly or moth egg hatches, the tiny worm-like larva, or caterpillar, crawls out and begins to eat.

Tight fit

As the caterpillar eats, it grows bigger but unlike most animals, its skin does not grow as the caterpillar grows. As it grows, the caterpillar's skin becomes too tight and it has to be shed. A split appears in the skin near the head. The caterpillar then wriggles out of the old skin. Molting usually happens several times in a caterpillar's life. In temperate regions, the caterpillar stage lasts for two to four weeks.

In cold climates, it can take two to three years for some caterpillars to change into butterflies.

Rings on legs

A caterpillar's body has thirteen rings, or segments, as well as a head. A pair of legs is attached to each of the first three segments. Each leg has five joints. On the **abdomen**, inside which food is digested, there are four or five pairs of softer legs, called **prolegs**. The head has six simple eyes on each side and a pair of pointed feelers or **antennae** that the caterpillar uses to guide itself along. To scare off predators, some caterpillars may be covered in hairs, bristles, or spines. Others have false eye-spots, or can squirt a liquid that stinks or burns.

Crawling caterpillar

poster board

pencil

scissors

gluestick

pipe cleaners

yarn

1 Draw and cut out two poster board rings, with smaller circles cut out inside them.

2 Put the two rings together and wind yard around them until the hole in the middle has disappeared.

3 Cut through the yarn between the two poster board circles.

4 Tie a piece of yarn between the rings and knot it. Leave a piece of yarn at both ends to attach to the next pompom.

5 Make five more colored pompoms. Cut out two small poster board circles for the eyes and glue them to the front pompom.

Make a friendly fluffy caterpillar to crawl across your floor

Glue on curled pipe cleaners to make the caterpillar's antennae.

Snail shells

Snails are a kind of **mollusk**, an animal with a soft body, usually protected by a hard shell. Snails are related to slugs. There are about 77,000 different species of snails and slugs that live throughout the world.

Homes that grow

Snails have a single spiral shell. When a snail is threatened, it can pull the soft part of its body inside the hard shell for protection. Other animals, such as crabs, have hard, or fixed, shells that have to be replaced as they grow. A snail's shell is part of its body and grows with the soft part.

Damp and dry spells

As a snail moves, it produces a sticky slime to help it slide across the ground. It moves its muscular 'foot' in a wave-like motion to propel itself forward on the slime.

Snails like dampness. In dry weather, the snail stays inside its shell, sealing itself in with a 'door' of dried slime. The snail stays inside the safety of its home until it rains again.

Shelly lid

Not all snails live on land. Many kinds, such as pond snails, live in water. Snails that live in the sea are called **marine** snails. Many types of marine snails have a 'lid', called an **operculum**, that seals off the snail whenever it draws itself inside its shell. The operculum stops predators from attacking and eating the snail. Marine snails often have very colorful or patterned shells. You can sometimes find these shells washed up on beaches.

Insects & Bugs

bowl

wooden spoon

cooking oil

baking tray

flour

paints

paint brush

glitter

glue

Patterned spirals

Make stunning shell spirals with bright paints and patterns

1 In a bowl, mix flour, water, and cooking oil into a dough. Add more flour if the dough is too sticky. Knead the dough, cover it, and put it in the fridge for half an hour.

2 Sprinkle some flour on a flat surface and roll the dough into long tubes.

3 Curl the tubes into spirals.

4 Place the spirals on a baking tray and bake them at 375°F for 30 minutes.

5 When cool, decorate your spirals with paint and glitter.

Beautiful butterfly

The butterfly is one of the most beautiful flying insects. It has two pairs of brightly colored or patterned wings. If you could look at the wings under a **microscope**, you would see that they are made of many tiny overlapping scales.

Butterfly bird

There are between 15,000 and 20,000 different species of butterflies in the world. The Queen Alexandra's birdwing has a wingspan as big as a bird's, while the western pygmy blue is smaller than a fingernail.

Colored wings

Butterflies come in all the colors of the rainbow. Some are bright, some are pale, and some have amazing patterns. Many have shimmering wings that change color when they move, as light reflects between each tiny wing scale.

Blending in

The color and pattern of a butterfly's wings help it to blend in among the flowers it feeds on, making it harder for enemies to see. It also helps the butterfly attract a mate. Some butterflies have wing patterns that look like, or mimic, bigger animals to scare off predators. The pearly eye butterfly has brown wings marked with spots that look like large eyes. The southern dogface has markings like a dog's face.

First flight

A new adult butterfly's wings are soft and crumpled at first. The veins running through them slowly fill with blood, and the wings are held out to dry. To fly, the butterfly uses its flight muscles to beat its wings and lift it up while the flexible edges bend and help push the butterfly forward.

Butterfly kite

WHAT YOU NEED

ball of string

paints and brush

paper

pencil

scissors

sequins and glitter

tape

two wooden sticks

glue

1

Fold a sheet of paper in half. Unfold, then draw half a butterfly shape.

2 Paint the half butterfly in bright, bold colors and patterns.

Decorate your butterfly in fantastic bold bright colors

3 With the paint still wet, fold the sheet over and rub gently with your hand. Open it up to see the entire symmetrical shape!

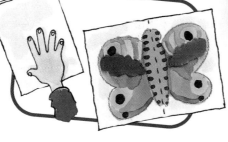

4 When dry, glue onto a second sheet and cut out.

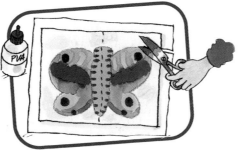

5 Tie the sticks in a cross, leaving a long string. Glue to the back of the butterfly.

6 Glue sequins and glitter on for decoration. Fly your kite on a windy day.

Fly's eyes

Have you ever tried to catch a housefly? It is usually walking or standing still. You can creep up on it very slowly, or try a fast grab, but almost every time, the fly is too quick and buzzes away out of reach. How does the fly see you coming?

Big eyes

A fly's eyes look tiny, but they are very large compared to its size. If the fly was as big as you, its eyes would be the size of footballs! They bulge from its head, so it can see almost all around, even behind its back.

TV vision

A television picture is made up of thousands of tiny dots or bars. From a distance, these merge together into one single scene. A fly sees the world like this, as thousands of tiny dots of light. This is because each eye is not a single part, but many tiny parts, called facets. The facets face outward, making the whole eye look like a bunch of pinheads. Each facet picks up, or detects, the light from one small part of a whole view.

On the move

Flies do not see with the same detail as humans do. They also do not see as many colors. The smallest movement changes the dot of light received by one facet and this is why flies always see you coming!

More bug-eyed bugs

It is not just flies that have multi-part, or compound, eyes. Beetles, dragonflies, butterflies, bees, and other insects have them too. Their eyes vary in size and the number of facets they have.

Insects & Bugs

Goggle-eye fly

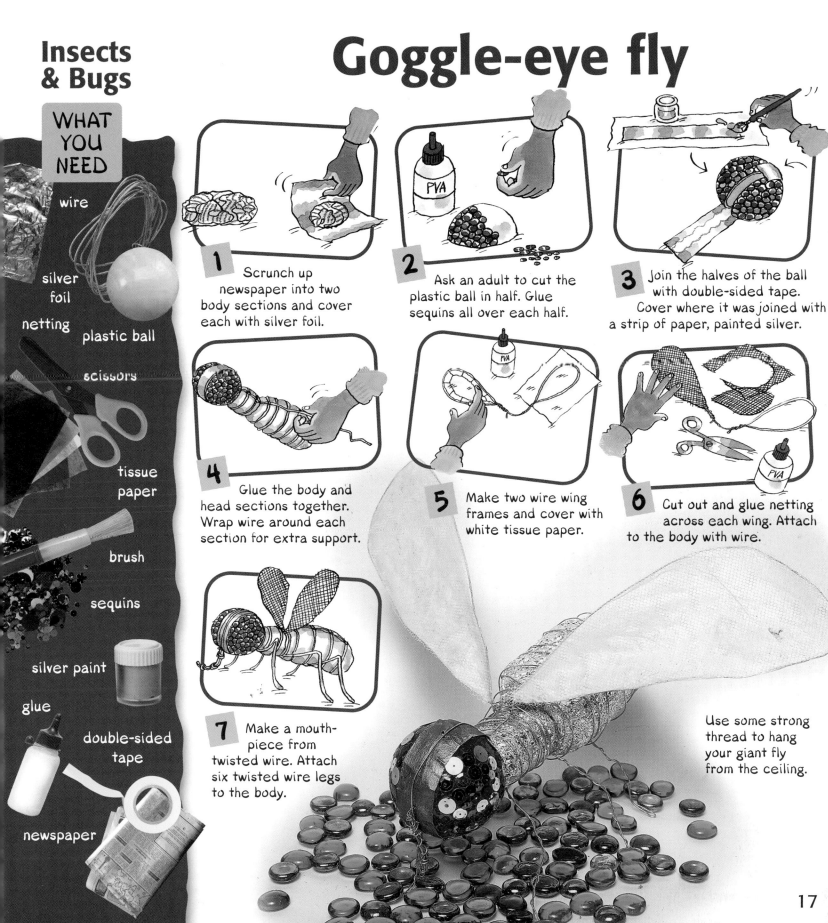

WHAT YOU NEED

- wire
- silver foil
- netting
- plastic ball
- scissors
- tissue paper
- brush
- sequins
- silver paint
- glue
- double-sided tape
- newspaper

1 Scrunch up newspaper into two body sections and cover each with silver foil.

2 Ask an adult to cut the plastic ball in half. Glue sequins all over each half.

3 Join the halves of the ball with double-sided tape. Cover where it was joined with a strip of paper, painted silver.

4 Glue the body and head sections together. Wrap wire around each section for extra support.

5 Make two wire wing frames and cover with white tissue paper.

6 Cut out and glue netting across each wing. Attach to the body with wire.

7 Make a mouth-piece from twisted wire. Attach six twisted wire legs to the body.

Use some strong thread to hang your giant fly from the ceiling.

A lot of legs

Centipedes and millipedes have more legs than any other animal. The word centipede means hundred-footed. It comes from centi meaning one hundred and pede which means feet. The word millipede means thousand-footed, from milli meaning one thousand. Millipedes do not have thousands of legs. The most they are known to have is 760 legs, or 380 pairs!

Joints and segments

The bodies of these worm-like **arthropods** are divided into segments, with jointed legs attached to each segment. Centipedes can have from 15 to 175 pairs of legs. Centipedes have one pair of legs attached to each body segment, but millipedes have two. There are more than 2,000 different species of centipedes and more than 8,000 different types of millipedes in the world. They range from the common garden millipede, just one-eighth of an inch (3 mm) long, to the giant desert centipede, that can be twelve inches (30 cm) long.

Poison jaws

Centipedes are very different from millipedes. The centipede is a fierce **carnivore** and a **cannibal**. Centipedes eat mollusks, worms, and other centipedes. Millipedes eat only plants.

The first pair of the centipede's legs are actually fangs. They are called **poison** jaws because they inject the prey with poison which comes from a gland in the centipede's head. Centipedes hunt at night and can run much faster than millipedes.

Self-defense

Millipedes and centipedes defend themselves against attackers in some surprising ways. The South African millipede squirts smelly chemicals from its skin, while the pill millipede rolls into a ball. All centipedes can afford to shed a few legs because they will soon grow back again.

This bright red centipede looks like a worm with legs!

Insects & Bugs

Smiling centipede

Make a rainbow-colored centipede with dangling dancing legs

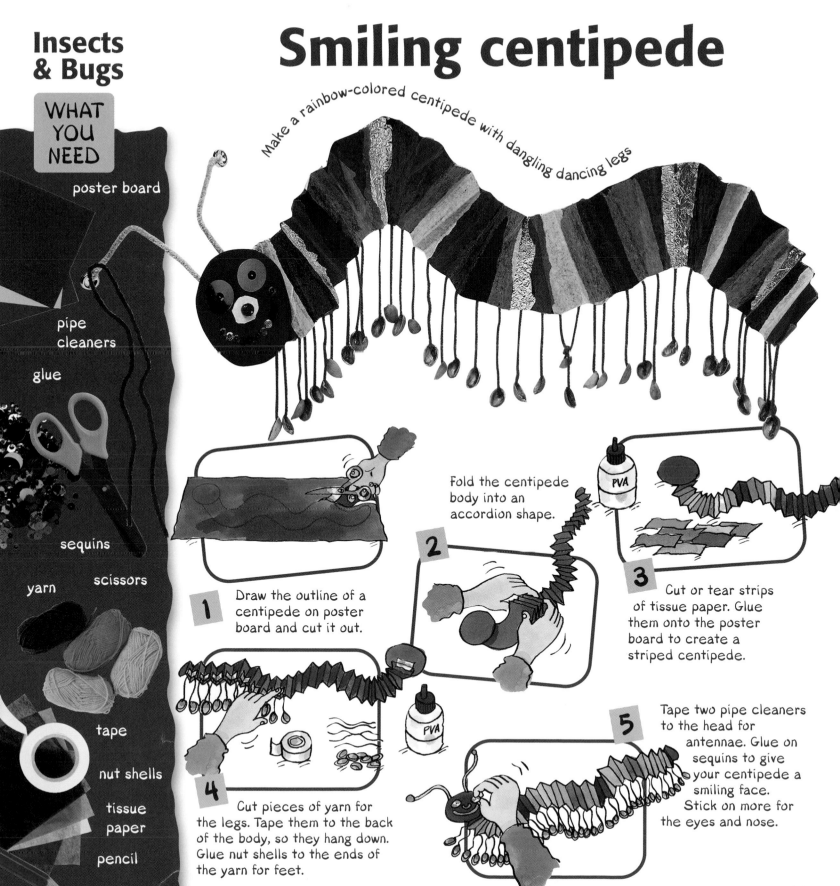

WHAT YOU NEED

poster board

pipe cleaners

glue

sequins

yarn

scissors

tape

nut shells

tissue paper

pencil

1 Draw the outline of a centipede on poster board and cut it out.

2 Fold the centipede body into an accordion shape.

3 Cut or tear strips of tissue paper. Glue them onto the poster board to create a striped centipede.

4 Cut pieces of yarn for the legs. Tape them to the back of the body, so they hang down. Glue nut shells to the ends of the yarn for feet.

5 Tape two pipe cleaners to the head for antennae. Glue on sequins to give your centipede a smiling face. Stick on more for the eyes and nose.

Little pests

Magnified image of a head louse clinging to a human hair.

Lousy louse

A louse has a flat body and curved claw legs to dig into skin or cling to hair. Most **lice** are smaller than a grain of rice and can drink more than five times their own weight in one blood meal. The female louse lays tiny pale eggs, called **nits**, and glues them to hairs or feathers.

Tiny animals called **parasites** love to drink blood. They stick their needle-sharp mouths through skin and suck up a nutritious meal. The animals they bite, including humans, are called their **hosts**.

Feasting fleas

Fleas are tiny insects, a bit bigger than a pinhead. They live on animals and people, hiding among hairs, fur, or feathers. At night, they crawl around sucking blood. All animals and birds have their own type of flea. If fleas cannot find their own hosts, cat and dog fleas, for example, may bite a person.

Itchy bites

Biting flies have thin sharp tube mouths that easily poke through skin. They do not live on a host, but visit for a take-out meal. Gnats and midges are the smallest blood-sucking flies. When a mosquito bites, it pumps special chemicals into the skin, so the bite swells into an itchy red bump.

Munching mites

Tiny pests called follicle mites live in our eyelids in the tiny pits, or follicles, the eyelashes grow from. They eat dead skin and oil in the follicle and are usually harmless.

Swelling tick

Mites are close cousins of spiders and so are ticks. A tick clings to its host with its beak-like mouth. As it sucks up 20 times its own weight in blood, it swells up to look like a red bean. After feeding, the tick, which is full of blood, drops off its host.

20

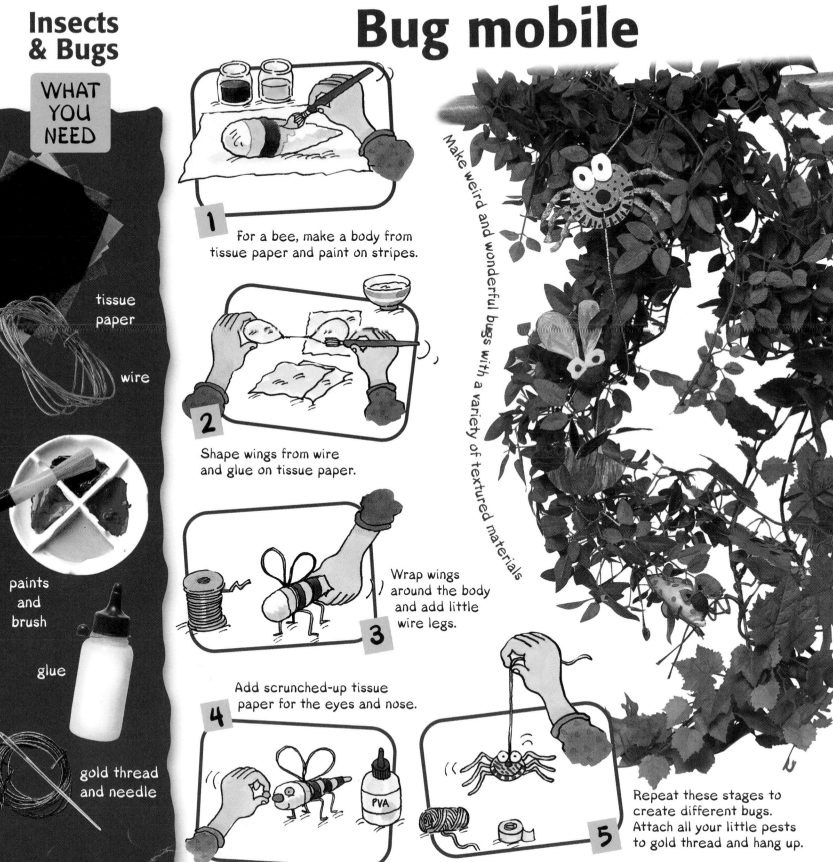

Insects & Bugs

WHAT YOU NEED

tissue paper

wire

paints and brush

glue

gold thread and needle

Bug mobile

Make weird and wonderful bugs with a variety of textured materials

1 For a bee, make a body from tissue paper and paint on stripes.

2 Shape wings from wire and glue on tissue paper.

3 Wrap wings around the body and add little wire legs.

4 Add scrunched-up tissue paper for the eyes and nose.

5 Repeat these stages to create different bugs. Attach all your little pests to gold thread and hang up.

Ants

Imagine being so strong that you could lift up a car. Imagine having to work all day and all night in a dark, damp, and crowded place. This is what ants do. For their size, ants are very strong. They can lift and carry pieces of leaves and twigs many times their own weight. Ants are also the busiest insects of all. They never take a rest from looking after their nest.

City in a hill

Some ants live in underground tunnels and some build mounds. Others live inside trees or plants, or make nests from leaves. An underground nest is protected on the outside by a mound of leaves, twigs, and soil. Inside is a maze of tunnels and rooms, called chambers, where more than 250,000 ants live. It is like a huge ant city.

The royal palace

Ants live together in large organized groups called colonies. Each colony has one or more queen ants. Only a queen ant lays eggs. One chamber in the nest is the "royal palace." This is the chamber where the queen ant lives. All the other ants are workers, with many different jobs to do.

Babysitter ants

Some worker ants are like babysitters. When the eggs are laid, they take them away to the "nursery" chambers in the nest. This is where the eggs hatch into grubs, or larvae. The babysitter ants feed and look after the young ants until they grow up and become worker ants themselves.

Busy workers

Other worker ants look after the nest. Some keep the tunnels and chambers clean inside, carrying away litter. Other workers repair any damage and build new tunnels or rooms. Workers travel away from the nest to defend it against enemies or to collect food. The defenders, or soldier ants, are the biggest workers with the largest jaws. A worker ant may have the same job all its life, or it may change tasks.

Marble ant maze

poster board

pencil

glue

scissors

sequins and star shapes

box lid

silver paint

marble

Roll your marble through the maze to the red spot

1 Draw the outline of a maze in your box lid and make a narrow opening at the start point.

2 Cut strips of poster board for the maze walls. Fold along the dotted lines.

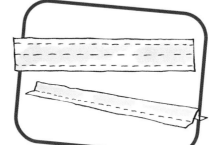

3 Glue the strips along the pencil lines.

4 When dry, paint the whole maze silver.

5 Decorate the maze walls with cut-up sequins.

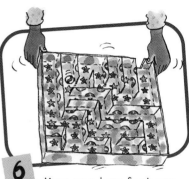

6 Now see how fast you can get the marble through the maze.

23

Paper homes

Wasps belong to a large group of insects called **hymenoptera**. Although some kinds of wasps live on their own, most live in large social groups known as colonies.

The colony has a queen. Only the queen wasp will mate and produce eggs. The other females are workers, while male wasps only visit to mate with the queen.

Pulp and paper

The queen chooses the nesting place that must be warm and dry. She uses her strong jaws to tear wood from twigs, fences, or even wooden beams. The queen then chews the wood into a soft pulp. This is used to build the nest and turns into a kind of paper when it dries. The queen builds the first cells, or comb. These are safe places where the young wasps will grow. When the first comb of five to ten cells is built, she lays one egg in each cell and glues it to the inside.

Silken cocoons

Twenty days later, the wasp larvae are large enough to fill their cells and begin to build a **cocoon** of silk thread. The queen builds a protective wall, called an envelope, around the cocoons. The wasps hatch after another twenty days. All of them are female. They help the queen to build more cells.

Multi-story combs

The female workers construct a new comb by joining it to the first with a pillar. As more wasps hatch, more combs and pillars are made and the bigger the nest grows. The very last cells to be made are bigger than the rest. They contain male wasps as well as other females that will become queens. These wasps leave the nest and mate. The males then die. The old queen and her workers stay with the nest until they die in the autumn.

Insects & Bugs

Queen wasp's nest

WHAT YOU NEED

egg cartons

paints and brush

wire

tissue paper

glue

paste

cotton balls

pipe cleaners

scissors

balloon

newspaper

1 Cut out the cups from the egg cartons and paint them pale yellow.

2 Glue the cups together in a honeycomb grid.

3 Stuff some of the cups with cotton balls.

4 Blow up the balloon into a small oval and paste on three layers of newspaper. When dry, pop the balloon.

5 Scrunch up a piece of tissue paper and glue it to the end for the head. Paint on yellow and black stripes and black eyes.

Stick pipe cleaners into the body for legs and into the head for antennae. Make wire wings. Stick them through the sides of the wasp's body.

Put the queen on the honeycomb and add some smaller worker wasps

25

Wiggly worms

Soft slimy earthworms soon dry up in the hot sun. That is why they live in the damp soil. They burrow through it, eating it as they go along and taking in **nutrients**. Leftover soil that the worm eats comes out as waste. This waste, called a cast, looks like a muddy squiggle. Earthworm tunnels are good for the soil because they let air and water in, mix up the layers, and help old leaves to rot. This keeps the soil fertile and plants healthy.

Worm wiggle

A worm's long body is made of many parts joined together, called segments. Its mouth is a hole at the pointed front end. A worm does not have legs, but it does have tiny hairs growing along its body. These hairs grip the sides of a worm's tunnel as it wriggles from side to side, squeezing through the soil.

Worms in danger!

Although worms have no ears or real eyes, the front part of a worm can tell whether it is light or dark. The worm's body can also detect, or feel, very tiny movements. For example, it can feel a bird hopping on the ground above, or an animal digging in the soil nearby. The worm will then tunnel deeper to get out of the way. If the worm's back end is bitten, it grows again. If the front end is damaged, the worm dies.

Parasites

Some species of worms are parasites. They live inside other animals and, sometimes, inside people. A tapeworm lives inside the gut or intestine of a larger animal, feeding on the soupy digested food around it. Roundworms live in the stomachs, muscles, intestines, and even in the eyes of other animals.

A friend to gardeners, the earthworm helps keep soil fertile.

Striped felt worm

WHAT
YOU
NEED

tissue
paper

needle

thread

sequins

gluestick

felt

beads

scissors

newspaper

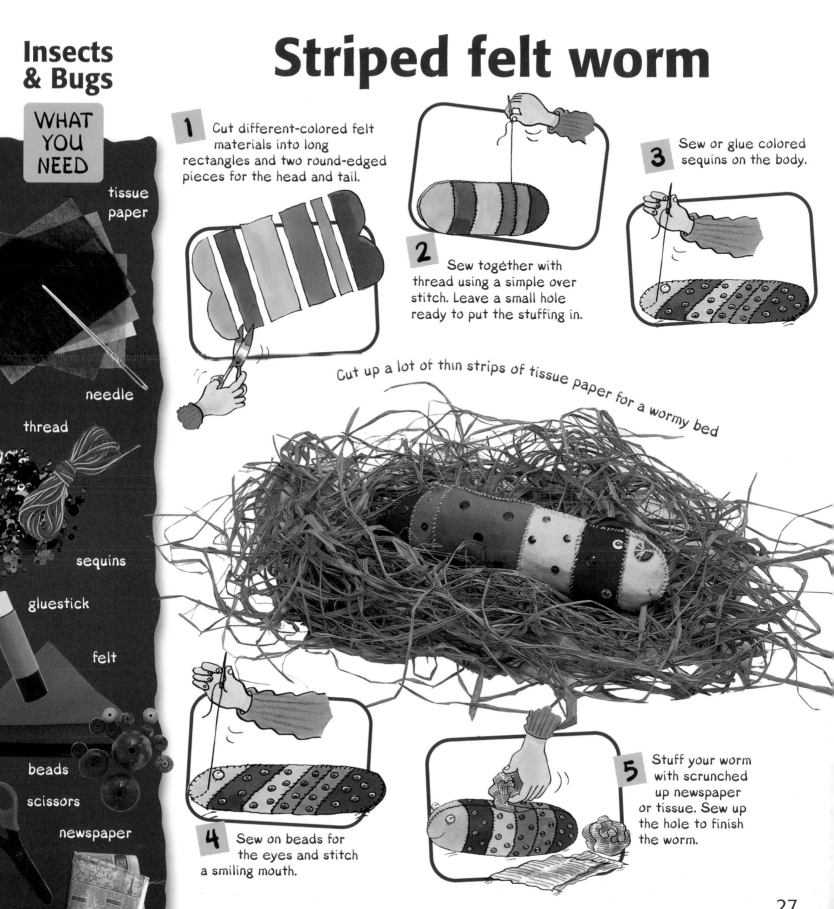

1 Cut different-colored felt materials into long rectangles and two round-edged pieces for the head and tail.

2 Sew together with thread using a simple over stitch. Leave a small hole ready to put the stuffing in.

3 Sew or glue colored sequins on the body.

Cut up a lot of thin strips of tissue paper for a wormy bed

4 Sew on beads for the eyes and stitch a smiling mouth.

5 Stuff your worm with scrunched up newspaper or tissue. Sew up the hole to finish the worm.

Magnificent moths

Have you ever watched moths fly around a light at night? Most moths are **nocturnal**, or night-time, relatives of butterflies. In fact, moths and butterflies are so alike that it can sometimes be difficult to tell them apart.

Growing up

Like butterflies, moths change their body shape as they grow up. They start life as an egg, that hatches into a caterpillar. The caterpillar then turns into an unmoving **pupa** from which, in a few weeks, a fully grown moth crawls out.

Butterfly or moth?

The main difference between moths and butterflies is that moths fly at night and butterflies feed in the daytime.

A bull's-eye moth displaying eye spots on its wings.

Another way of telling moths and butterflies apart is by seeing how they hold their wings when resting. Moths rest with their wings out flat, while butterflies usually hold their wings upright.

Camouflage

Most moths are less colorful than butterflies, to blend in better with their surroundings. Many have leaf-like or bark patterns on their wings. These help to **camouflage**, or disguise them, while resting in a tree. Some moths have brightly colored wings that are just as beautiful as a butterfly's. These moths are usually poisonous or bad-tasting! Others frighten away predators because they have large spots on their wings that look like, or mimic, eyes.

Friend or pest?

Moths pollinate many flowers. When they feed on a flower's nectar, pollen sticks to the moth's furry body and rubs off onto other flowers it visits. The caterpillars of silkworm moths produce silk thread that they weave into a case, called a cocoon, to protect the pupa. The thread can be unwound and spun into valuable silk fabric. The hungry caterpillars or larvae of many moths are considered pests. They munch their way through crops, or even wool clothing, leaving holes behind.

Velvet moth

Put your hand inside the glove and flap the wings of your moth

WHAT YOU NEED

needle and thread

sequins

scissors

fabric   velvet

beads

glue

braid

pipe cleaners

1 Cut out two hand-sized pieces of fabric for the moth's body, as shown.

2 Stitch the two pieces together, inside out. Leave the base open.

3 Cut wings and central body flaps out of velvet and fabric. Decorate with patches and sequins.

4 Turn the body right-side out and stitch on the wings. Glue pipe cleaners on the head for antennae.

5 Sew two beads onto the face for the eyes. Add the braid.

You can use different materials to make striped, checked, or patchwork moths.

29

Jeweled webs

Silk spinners

Spiders produce silk from special glands inside their abdomen. The glands make the liquid silk, which is then squeezed out through six **spinnerets** at the tip of the abdomen. Each spinner squirts out the silk in long sticky threads.

A pretty trap

The large circular orb web is the biggest and most complicated web shape. It takes about an hour for the orb web spider to spin its web. It usually does this at night, or just before dawn. First, the spider makes the frame, stretching strands of silk between trees or flower stems. Strands of silk are then stretched from the center, like the spokes of a wheel. Finally, the spider weaves the silk in between each spoke in a spiral shape. The insect trap is complete!

Web wonders

Not all webs are the same. Funnel-web spiders spin a silk tube that ends in a flat sheet. The spider hides in the bottom of the tube. When an insect lands on the sheet, the spider rushes out and stabs it, then drags it down to its **lair**. Scaffold-web spiders spin the simplest webs. These are usually just a tangle of silky threads stuck to one point, such as the corner of a ceiling. The net-casting spider goes fishing for its prey. It spins a web between its back legs and uses its front legs to throw it over prey passing on the ground.

Have you ever watched a spider making a web? Have you ever seen a small insect struggling to escape from the web's sticky strands? Spiders are master spinners and weavers who spin silk threads to catch insects for food. Some spiders do not need a web to catch their prey.

Insects & Bugs

WHAT YOU NEED

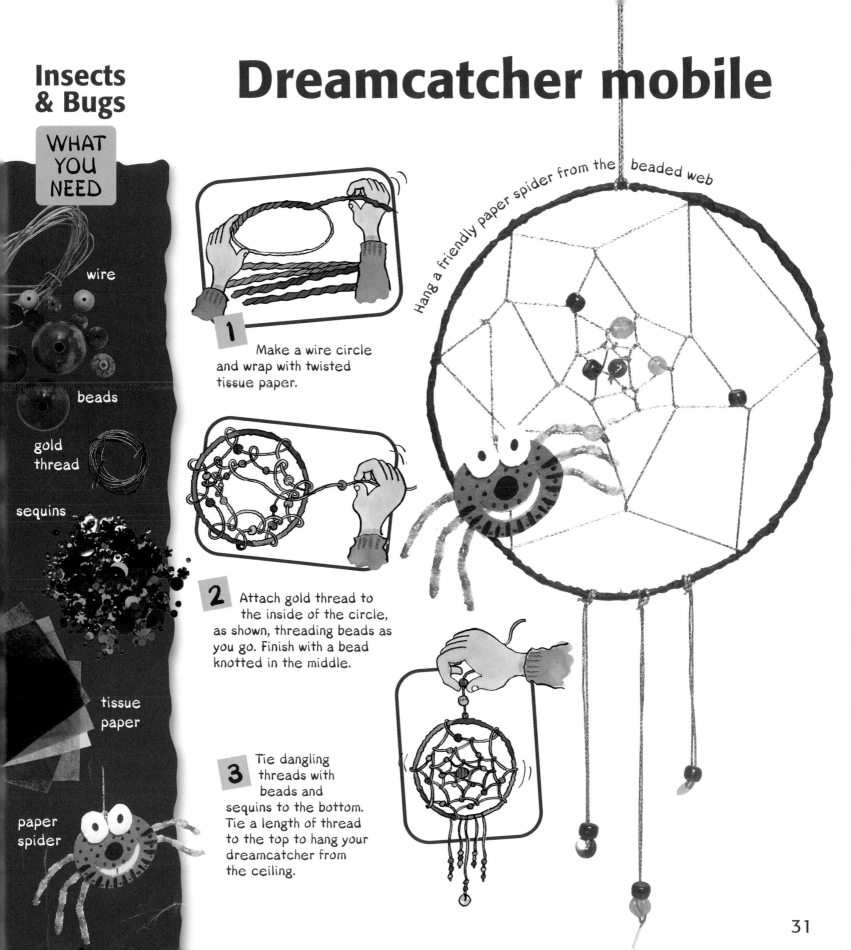

wire

beads

gold thread

sequins

tissue paper

paper spider

1 Make a wire circle and wrap with twisted tissue paper.

2 Attach gold thread to the inside of the circle, as shown, threading beads as you go. Finish with a bead knotted in the middle.

3 Tie dangling threads with beads and sequins to the bottom. Tie a length of thread to the top to hang your dreamcatcher from the ceiling.

Hang a friendly paper spider from the beaded web

Shield bugs

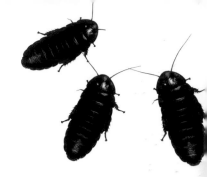

Surviving in nature is like surviving a battle. This is why many insects and bugs have hard thick shells, or coverings, over their bodies. This armor protects them from predators, such as birds, and from bad weather, falling twigs, and other dangers.

Tough pest

One of the toughest bugs is the cockroach. Cockroaches live almost everywhere in the world. The cockroach's flat body is protected with a tough covering like stiff leather, called an exoskeleton. Long strong legs help the cockroach to race or climb away from danger. Some types of cockroaches can fly. Cockroaches breed fast and are difficult to kill. They eat almost anything, from leftover food to the droppings of other **pests,** such as rats and mice.

Shield-shaped

A shieldbug's hard flat body is shaped just like the shield of a medieval knight. The green shieldbug is the same color as the leaves it lives on, so predators cannot see it easily.

Strong wings

Like most other insects, beetles have four wings. The first two are tough dome-shaped cases that are curved and very strong. Together, these wings cover most of the beetle's body. They also protect the thin delicate second wings that are folded underneath.

Armor plates

Another armor-plated insect is the woodlouse. The woodlouse's body has about twelve wide curved plates that look like strips of armor.

Robot beetle

1 Draw the shapes on poster board as shown, and cut them out.

2 Paint both cut-out shapes silver, and glue glitter to the long strip.

3 Make folds in the long piece, as shown, and glue ends together.

4 Decorate the rounded cut-out with sequins, wire, and glitter. Glue onto the base.

5 Cut out six wheels from the thick cardboard and paint or color.

6 Poke the three sticks through the base and push on the wheels.

Glue on the plastic top. Add sequins for eyes and pipe-cleaner antennae.

Design and make all kinds of armor-plated robot insects

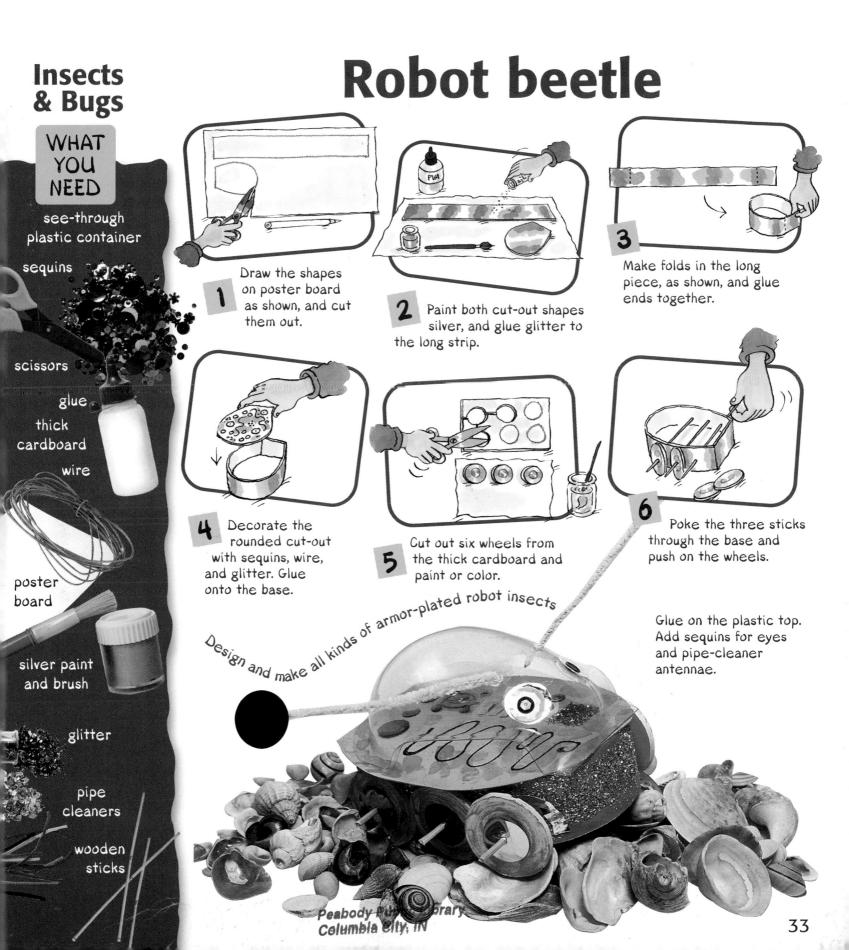

Hoppers and hunters

Leg work

Grasshoppers, crickets, and mantids have six legs, like other insects. The back two legs of grasshoppers and crickets are much longer and stronger than the others. These legs are usually folded in an upside-down V against the sides of the body. To jump, the grasshopper pulls its back feet forward, bringing the folded leg parts together. Its leg muscles jerk fast and hard, straightening the leg and flinging the grasshopper into the air. As well as hopping around to find food and a mate, grasshoppers and crickets use their powerful kick to escape predators, such as birds and lizards, or leap away in a flash.

Hunting tools

Mantids have stronger front legs, designed for killing, not jumping! They are a mantid's hunting tool, and are lined with sharp spines for grabbing and holding prey. The mantid's other four legs are thinner and are used for walking and holding onto twigs.

Some insects use their powerful legs to do hard tasks. Grasshoppers and crickets are the champion hoppers of the insect world. They can leap about 200 times their own length! Mantids, some of the fiercest predators of the insect world, use their strong front legs to strike out at their prey with lightning-fast speed.

Chirp-chirp

Quickly rub your fingernail across the teeth of a plastic comb. The zip-zip-zip sound you hear is similar to the sound of singing crickets. Male grasshoppers and crickets sing to attract females of their kind for **breeding**. Most grasshoppers sing by rubbing a hard ridge on their flap-like front wings along a row of tiny knobs on their back legs. Crickets rub together the spiky veins on their two front wings.

34

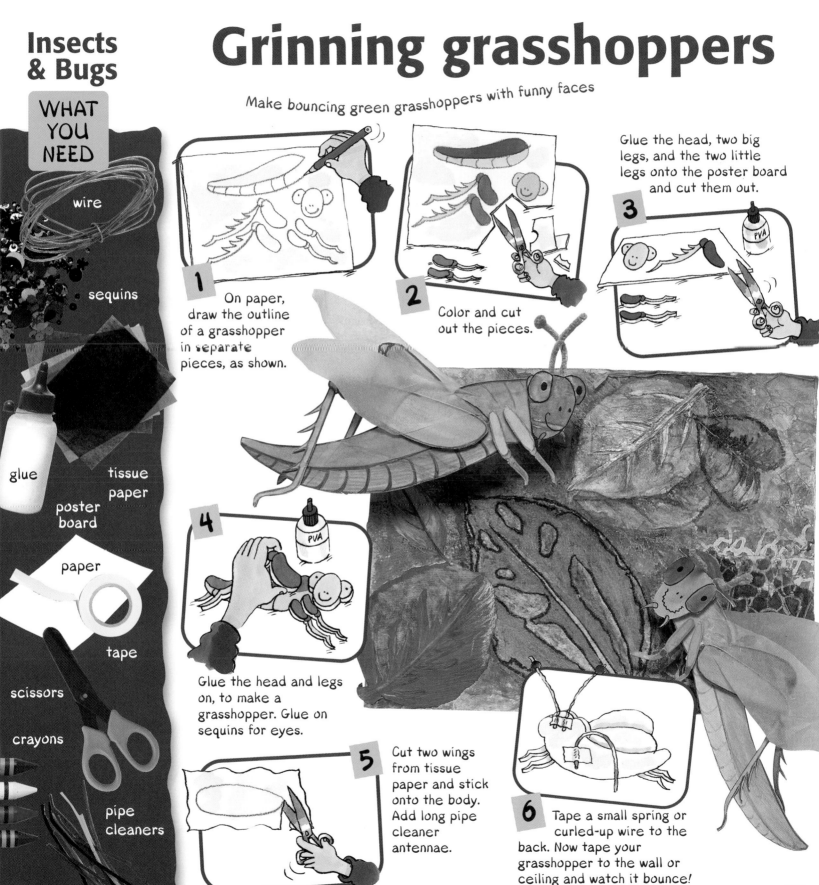

Insects & Bugs

WHAT YOU NEED

wire

sequins

glue

tissue paper

poster board

paper

tape

scissors

crayons

pipe cleaners

Grinning grasshoppers

Make bouncing green grasshoppers with funny faces

1 On paper, draw the outline of a grasshopper in separate pieces, as shown.

2 Color and cut out the pieces.

3 Glue the head, two big legs, and the two little legs onto the poster board and cut them out.

4 Glue the head and legs on, to make a grasshopper. Glue on sequins for eyes.

5 Cut two wings from tissue paper and stick onto the body. Add long pipe cleaner antennae.

6 Tape a small spring or curled-up wire to the back. Now tape your grasshopper to the wall or ceiling and watch it bounce!

Stick thin

Camouflage champions

Stick insects are also called walking sticks, phasmids, specter, or ghost insects. Their long thin bodies and legs are usually green or brown in color and they look exactly like sticks or twigs. Predators, such as birds, do not notice them because they are so well camouflaged. Not only are stick insects shaped and colored like twigs or stems, but their bodies also have small ridges, lumps, bumps, or spikes, just like the bark and twigs all around them.

Raining eggs

At breeding time, each female stick insect lays her eggs by letting them fall to the ground, one-by-one. If many stick insects are laying, the falling eggs sound like the patter of rain. The eggs look like plant seeds and usually hatch after a year. After they hatch, the young stick insects, called nymphs, crawl up the nearest tree and begin munching leaves.

The stick insect really looks like its name! Can you tell where it is?

At sunset in a tropical forest, many animals settle down to sleep. This is also the time when a lot of other animals wake up and feed. In the daytime, stick insects stay very still and hide in bushes and trees. When stick insects wake up at night, they move very slowly, feeding on leaves and buds. There are so many stick insects it looks as if hundreds of twigs and stems have come alive.

Fighting back

Stick insects protect themselves in many ways. They sometimes surprise predators by folding up their legs and falling to the ground, or opening their bright rear wings to show a sudden flash of color. They also vomit smelly half-digested food, kick with their spiky legs, or squirt a stinky stinging liquid.

Stick insect parade

pipe cleaners

glue

brush

green paint

sequins

small plant

1 Paint 20 to 30 pipe cleaners using different shades of green paint. Leave them to dry.

2 Make the insect's legs by wrapping three pipe cleaners around one central pipe cleaner. This will be the insect's body.

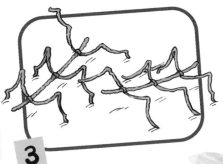

3 Bend the legs and body to make the insects stand in different poses. Glue on sequin eyes.

Stick insects are masters of disguise. Can you spot them in the leaves?

Hide your insects among stems and leaves

37

Wood whittlers

The young, or larvae, of wood-boring beetles are expert wood carvers. They spend their time chewing through wood, making tunnels as they eat. Throughout its **life cycle**, a beetle changes shape four times, in a process called **metamorphosis.** It starts life as an egg and hatches into a larva before becoming a pupa. Finally, an adult beetle emerges.

Hungry burrowers

Wood-boring beetles, such as deathwatch and bark beetles, lay their eggs just under the bark of trees, or under wooden materials. When the eggs hatch, the larvae burrow down into the wood, where they are surrounded by food and are safe from hungry predators. They stay there until they become fully grown beetles. Most adult beetles then crawl out and start feeding on a different type of food, such as flower pollen. Some carry on eating wood as adults.

Drilling and boring

Beetle larvae use their chewing mouthparts to drill tunnels in front of them. If there are beetle larvae in bark or wood, you can see the tiny sawdust trails coming out from the tunnels that they have bored. You can also see the holes left by the full-grown beetles when they leave their woody homes.

Little pests

Many wood-boring beetles or their larvae are pests, causing serious damage to buildings, furniture, or trees. The larvae of the elm bark beetle spread Dutch elm disease that kills elm trees by carrying a fungus from tree to tree. In houses, the deathwatch beetle can turn timber beams into skeletons. This beetle prefers wood that is more than 100 years old. Many historic buildings have been ruined by this hungry beetle's tunneling.

A close-up of the tunnels left by wood-boring beetles under tree bark.

Wood sculpture

gold thread

corks

bamboo

pine cones

scrapwood or other kinds of wood

brush

glue

wire

varnish

wood shavings

1 Arrange your pieces of wood, cork, and bamboo so they criss-cross in an attractive design. Glue in place.

2 Hang corks, pine cones, and other bits and pieces from the bamboo sticks using thread or wire.

Find materials in the garden, woods, or at the beach

3 Brush parts of your sculpture with varnish to help create different textures and shades. (Ask an adult to help you.)

Termite towers

Imagine a gigantic skyscraper with a busy city inside it. The skyscraper city has hundreds of rooms, food stores, a large nursery, and an air-conditioning system! This is what it is like in a termite tower.

Sky high

Termites live in groups, called colonies, in hot dry parts of the world. They protect their nest by building a tower on top of it, which is sometimes more than twenty feet (6 m) high. If termites were the same size as people, their towers would be six times higher than the world's tallest skyscrapers!

Soil city

Termites usually make the tower from soil that they shape by chewing and moistening it. When the soil dries, it is as hard as brick. Inside the tower, tubes, called chimneys, let air flow up from the underground nest, keeping it cool and damp. The tower not only protects the termites from drying out in the sun, but also from many predators, including ants, lizards, birds, and anteaters.

Busy workers

Termites are blind and live underground nearly all their lives. Termite workers have different jobs. Some gather food, some guard the nest, while others take away trash or repair the tower. Babysitter workers have the important task of looking after the eggs, which are laid only by the bigger queen termite. The queen lays twenty eggs every minute for about five years. As soon as an egg hatches, the young termite begins work.

Insects & Bugs

WHAT YOU NEED

toilet paper rolls

paste

newspaper

cardboard

tissue paper

paints and paint brush

glue

straws

bottle caps

plastic spoons and lid

Junk tower

1 Glue the toilet paper roll to a square piece of cardboard.

2 Scrunch up newspaper and glue around the tube, building up the shape of a termite tower.

3 Paste on layers of tissue paper.

4 Glue junk, such as bottle caps, straws, plastic spoons, or wooden sticks, onto your tower.

Make termite models for your tower

Now paint it a bright color

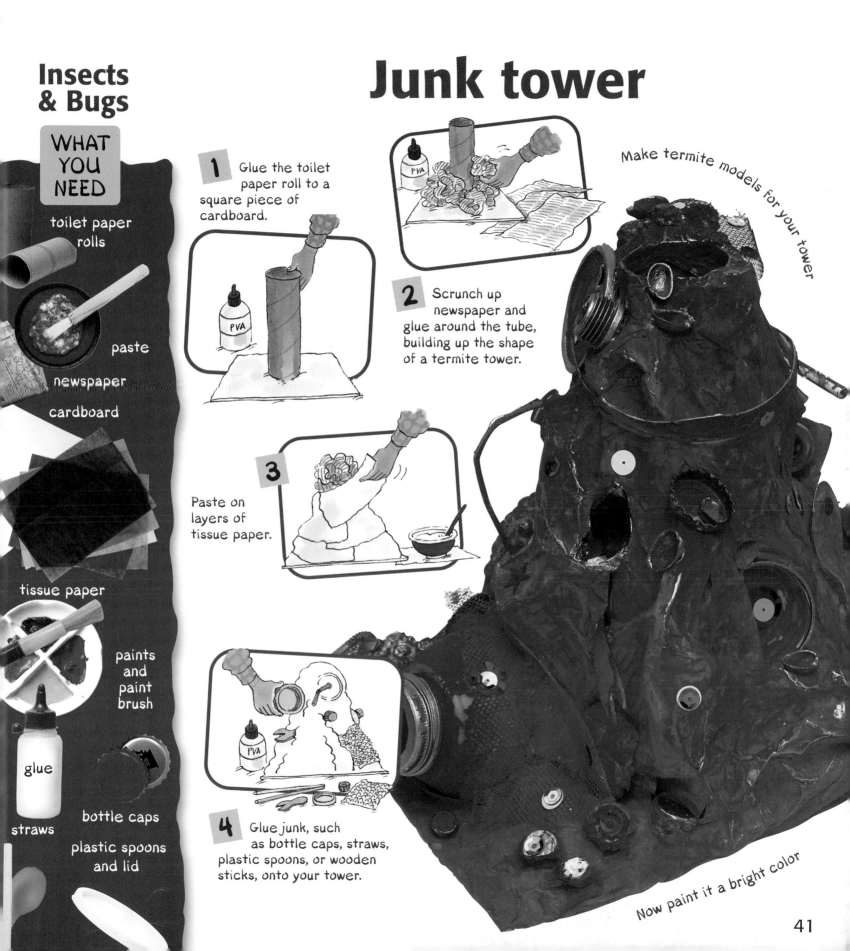

Rowers and skaters

D̶o you wish you could run on water, or swim as fast as a speedboat? Some insects can. Pondskaters scoot across the surface of water, while backswimmers and water-boatmen row along at amazing speeds.

Staying on top

The pondskater is a very small light insect. The pondskater's light weight, and the brush-like hairs on the bottom of its feet that trap tiny bubbles of air, help it to stay afloat. To skate across the water, a pondskater uses its long middle legs like a pair of oars and steers with its back legs. Pondskaters can feel the ripples sent out across the water's surface by a struggling insect. These tell the pondskater which way to skid and slide to find its meal.

Upside-down hunter

The backswimmer hangs just underneath the water's surface. Like the pondskater, the backswimmer feels the ripples made by struggling prey. It rows over at top speed, jerking its big rear legs forward and backward like oars.

On the bottom

A water-boatman looks similar to a backswimmer, but it lives on the bottom of the pond. The water-boatman rows through the water using its paddle shaped back legs, clings to weeds with its middle legs, and scoops up plants with its front legs.

Rowing boat

large plastic bottle

glue

masking tape

scissors

acrylic paints and brush

sequins and star shapes

corrugated cardboard

tin foil

eight wooden sticks

1 Cut the ends off a bottle and cut the tube in half lengthwise.

2 Cut two shapes from the discarded half, as shown. Join them onto each end of the base with masking tape.

3 Paint your boat and decorate with shiny sequins or star shapes.

Slide the oars onto your boat and display it on a wavy surface of blue netting

4 Ask an adult to make four holes in each side of the boat for the oars.

5 Cut eight paddle shapes from corrugated cardboard and paint them. Glue a paddle to one end of each stick.

6 Glue foil around the other end. Varnish your boat with PVA glue mixed with a little water.

Nightlights

The glowing light trail left by a flashing firefly.

On a warm clear summer's evening, just as it is beginning to get dark, you might see a small bright light dart suddenly across the sky. The light is a firefly. Fireflies are a type of small beetle, whose body glows with a yellow light. The light is made by a special substance, called **luciferin,** in the firefly's skin.

Cold glow

When an electric lightbulb shines, it gets hot. A firefly's glow is a cold light. Other animals make their own light too. The flashlight fish is the brightest light-maker. Its light can be seen from 98 feet (30 m) away.

Flashing codes

Fireflies glow in the dark to find a mate. The males fly around, flashing their lights on and off. The females sit on nearby twigs and bushes and flash their own lights in reply. Each species, or kind, of firefly has its own code of flashes. This way, the males and females recognize their own kind and can get together to breed.

Glowing worm

Glow-worms are another kind of beetle that shines in the dark. In the evening, the wingless female crawls up a stem or twig and twists herself around to show the light shining from her rear underside, or abdomen. Male glow-worms do not have a light. They fly around, looking for the shining females, so they can breed.

44

Insects & Bugs

WHAT YOU NEED

black poster board

silver and gold paints

tissue paper

brush

gluestick

glitter

gold thread

wire

tape

sequins

Firefly sky

1 Decorate a piece of black poster board with glitter, sequins, and metallic paints.

2 Scrunch the tissue paper into round body shapes and into tiny round balls for eyes.

3 Make wire wing shapes and cover with tissue paper.

4 Glue the wings around the tissue paper bodies. Stick on the tiny tissue paper eyes.

5 Spread glue over the bodies and dip them into glitter.

Hang glittery glowing fireflies against a night sky

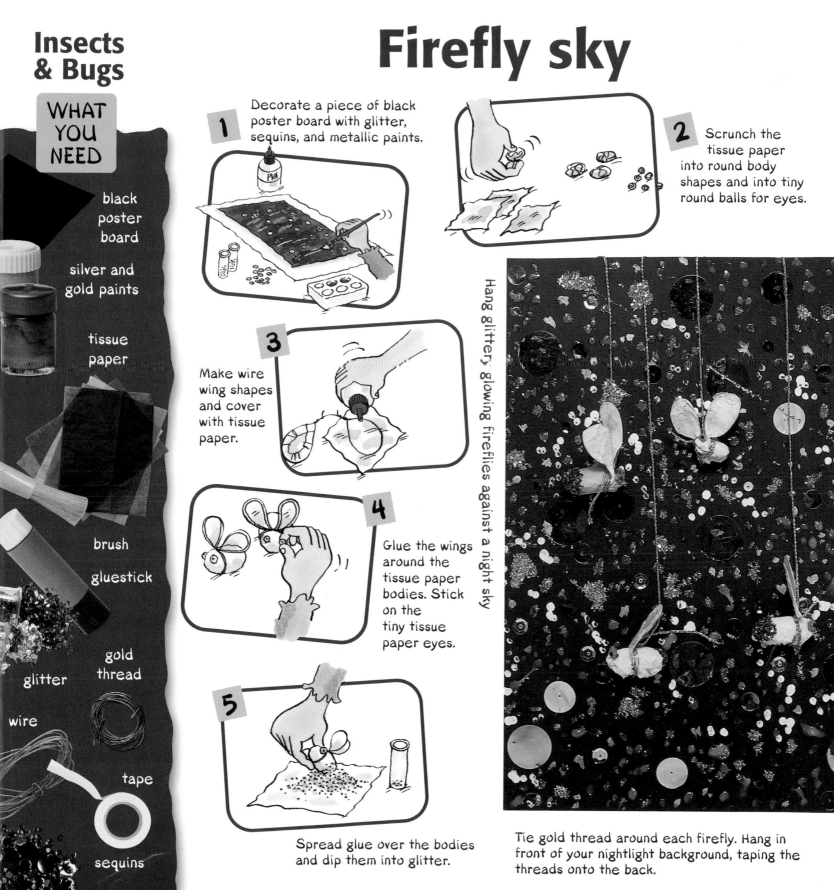

Tie gold thread around each firefly. Hang in front of your nightlight background, taping the threads onto the back.

Glossary

abdomen The rear section of an insect's body.

antennae A pair of sensitive feelers on an insect's head. Insects sense things about their surroundings by smell, taste, and touch, and their antennae help them do this. One of these is called an antenna.

aphids Small insects that feed by sucking the juices from plants.

arthropods Animals with jointed legs and body segments, such as insects and spiders.

breeding Producing babies.

camouflage The patterns or colors on an animal's skin that allow it to hide without being seen.

cannibal An animal that eats members of its own species.

carnivore A meat-eating animal.

cocoon A case made of silken threads that protects the pupae of insects, such as butterflies.

colonies Groups of the same type of animals or plants that live or grow together.

comb The regular shaped chambers that make up the nest of wasps and bees.

compound eyes Eyes that are made up of hundreds of different parts called facets. Each facet has a tiny lens on its surface.

drones Male bees whose only job is to mate with the queen bee.

exoskeleton The tough outer casing of an arthropod's body. The exoskeleton protects the body parts under it.

facets The tiny parts of a fly's eye that are able to detect the movement of light.

glands Parts of the body that produce special substances, such as venom or wax.

grubs A term used to describe the larvae of many insects, especially beetles.

hatches Emerges, or breaks out of, an egg.

hibernate To spend the winter in a sleep-like state. This helps many animals survive the cold of the winter months.

hosts Animals that a parasite feeds and lives on or in.

hymenoptera The name given to a group of insects that includes wasps and bees.

insects Arthropods with six legs and a body that is divided into three parts – head, thorax, and abdomen.

lair An animal's den or home.

larvae Young insects that are different when they become adults. One of these is called a larva.

lice Wingless bloodsucking insects. One of these is called a louse.

life cycle The series of body changes that happen in the life of an animal or plant.

luciferin A substance present in the bodies of fireflies that glows with a yellowish light.

marine Found in, or relating to, the sea.

metamorphosis The rapidly changing growth stages of the larvae of certain animals into the adult form.

microscope An instrument that makes things appear larger.

mimic To copy the behavior, or take on the appearance, of another animal.

mollusk A soft-bodied invertebrate such as a snail.

molts To shed, or get rid of, hair, feathers, or old skin.

nectar A sugary liquid produced by flowers. Bees and other insects feed on nectar and pick up pollen that they then take to other flowers.

nits The eggs of a louse.

nocturnal Animals that are active at night, such as moths.

nutrients Substances that nourish an animal or plant.

nymph The larva of an insect such as a grasshopper.

operculum A door or lid attached to the foot of a marine snail for closing its shell.

parasites Animals, such as fleas, that live and feed on, or inside, another animal.

pests Insects that damage crops, or injure livestock.

poison Any substance that can cause damage or injury to the body, or even kill.

pollen Tiny powdery grains made by the male parts of a flower. Seeds are formed when the pollen reaches the female parts of the flower. Bees and insects carry pollen between flowers and this is called pollination.

predators Animals that hunt and kill other animals for food.

prey Animals that are hunted and eaten by other animals.

prolegs Pairs of soft legs on a caterpillar's body.

pupa The stage at which an insect larva changes into an adult insect.

royal jelly A substance made by worker bees that is fed to all young bee larvae, and fed continuously throughout the development of larvae that become queen bees.

species A particular type of plant or animal. Members of the same species can mate and produce young.

spinnerets The tubes at the end of a spider's abdomen, through which it squeezes silk threads to make its web.

Index

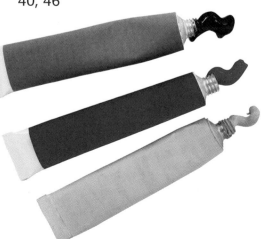

Materials guide

A list of materials, how to use them, and suitable alternatives

The crafts in this book require the use of materials and products that are easily purchased in craft stores. If you cannot locate some materials, you can substitute other materials with those we have listed here, or use your imagination to make the craft with what you have on hand.

Gold foil: can be found in craft stores. It is very delicate and sometimes tears.

Silver foil: can be found in craft stores. It is very delicate, soft and sometimes tears. For some crafts, tin or aluminum foil can be substituted. Aluminum foil is a less delicate material and makes a harder finished craft.

PVA glue: commonly called polyvinyl acetate. It is a modeling glue that creates a type of varnish when mixed with water. It is also used as a strong glue. In some crafts, other strong glues can be substituted, and used as an adhesive, but not as a varnish.

Filler paste: sometimes called plaster of Paris. It is a paste that hardens when it dries. It can be purchased at craft and hardware stores.

Paste: a paste of 1/2 cup flour, one tablespoon of salt and one cup of warm water can be made to paste strips of newspaper as in a papier mâché craft. Alternatively, wallpaper paste can be purchased and mixed as per directions on the package.

Cellophane: a clear or colored plastic material. Acetate can also be used in crafts that call for this material. Acetate is a clear, or colored, thin plastic that can be found in craft stores.

labels: gold foil / silver foil / filler paste / PVA glue / flour / salt / cellophane or acetate

   1 2 3 4 5 6 7 8 9 0   Printed in the USA 0 9 8 7 6 5 4 3 2